MONKEY

Hero of Our Time

igloobooks

Published in 2013
by Igloo Books Ltd
Cottage Farm
Sywell
NN6 0BJ
www.igloobooks.com

Additional images supplied courtesy of Thinkstock, Getty Images.

HUN001 0913
2 4 6 8 10 9 7 5 3
ISBN 978-1-78197-458-2

Printed and manufactured in China

MONKEY

Hero of Our Time

igloobooks

I dedicate this to
my best friend, me.

–*Contents*–

– Foreword –

"I've been very lucky to have someone like Monkey in my life. He's been a constant inspiration to me since the very first time we met."

AI.

I was working as a waitress in a cocktail bar, when I met... Wait, hold on, that's not right. That's a line from a song, I think. No, I was working as a door-to-door salesman, flogging dusters, when I knocked on a certain door one day. The door opened, but I couldn't see anyone. So I looked down.

There he was – Monkey. Our eyes met and as he looked me up and down and tutted. The connection between us was instant.

It was as though we were long-lost brothers that had been reunited at that very moment. Or even twins, separated at birth. Although, not identical twins, obviously.

Since that incredible day, Monkey has been my best friend, my confidant, my spiritual guide and my harshest critic. Sometimes he makes me sit on the naughty step, which seems a bit unfair, but he says it's for the best. What's more unfair is that I have to sit there for one minute for every year I've been alive, which can be hard, especially as we've got wooden stairs and he doesn't let me sit on a cushion!

But he's definitely made me into a better person and those days of trudging around selling dusters door-to-door every day are long gone. Now I get to do it online instead.

Monkey asked me to write the foreword to his sensational autobiography, even though he could have got one of his showbiz pals like Johnny Depp, Gwyneth Paltrow or Vernon Kay to do it instead. But as Monkey said himself, "You'll do it for free, won't you?'"

He was right.

I love him and even if you're undecided now, by the time you've finished reading this book, you will as well.

Probably.

Hopefully.

Al

WE LOVE T

THE GLORY DAYS '96

COSY NIGHT IN 1999

ERR, WHO'S ACTUALLY
TAKING ALL THESE PHOTOS

9

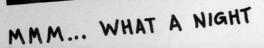

MMM... WHAT A NIGHT

–Chapter One–

Introducing Me

Picture the scene. A high-class London eatery one evening back in 2005. I'm in my favourite window seat, knocking back a smoothie made from the four most expensive things on the menu and enjoying the banter with some of my A-list showbiz chums – Jeremy Clarkson, Denise Welch and Jamiroquai.

A face appears, peering in through the glass. A haunted face. A stubbled face. I need to look twice, nay thrice, before I realise it is my old friend, Gary Barlow. I shudder. "Monkey," he mouths through the window. "Do you think I should try and get Take That back together?"

I go to the doorway (there would be no chance of him being allowed entry) and say, "Yes, Gary. You should do that, as soon as is physically possible," before handing him ten pounds to spend on top-up credit for his pay-as-you-go phone, allowing him to make the all-important calls.

Before he trudges off into the cold, unforgiving night, I ask, "Is there anything else I can do for you, Gary?" He replies, "Just one thing, Monkey. Please, *please,* write your autobiography. The world needs to hear your story."

Rewind back to 1995. I'm about to hit the red carpet at some award ceremony, or other, when a young lady thrusts a manuscript into my hand. It is called *Harry Popper and the Philosopher's Cheeses*.

When I get home I read it in one go. The next day, I ring JK and tell her that, with a couple of minor changes, she could have a world-shattering best-seller on her hands.

The rest, of course, is history. A couple of years later, I bumped into JK in a jacuzzi in a nine-star hotel in St. Tropez. Naturally, she was a billionaire by then and it was all thanks to my sound advice.

"Monkey," she said, as we clinked two glasses of strawberry milkshake together, "I'm so grateful for all your help, but I need another favour from you."

I would make a good popper →

HARRY POPPER AND THE PHILOSOPHER'S CHEESES

How about 'Potter'?

Original story by

J K Rowling

Sometimes if I've run out of cheese I use 'stone'.
You should try it!

First Draft
Revised: Mar 14, 1990

"I've got six more Harry Popper books planned," she still calls him that to this day, "and I'd really like them to do well, but I've heard that you're planning to publish your autobiography. If you do, it could put the rest of us authors out of business, as it would obviously be the most amazing book written in the history of everything, ever. Do you think you could wait for a few years?"

She's a good kid, so I agreed.

It isn't just celebrities that have clamoured for me to commit my life story to paper. For years now, strangers have sidled up to me in the street, the supermarket and in the queue for the ice-cream van, all with the same question.

"Monkey, when are you going to write your autobiography? Katie Price has done about *eight* of them and you're almost as important as she is," they all say. Or words to that effect.

Well, people, this is it. The real story, warts and all!

I've decided that it's finally time that the truth was told and there's only one small, woolly guy for the job.

Me of course.

Well, people, this is it. The real story, warts and all!

For years now,
I've tried to
cling on tightly
to my privacy..

… only letting the rest of the world get a glimpse of my life via a handful of carefully chosen television appearances.

Yes, of course I've also turned up at hundreds of film premieres, appeared in dozens of magazine photo features and been interviewed by most of the world's top journalists. However, I've always tried to hold a very important part of the real me back at the same time.

In a way, what has looked like a rampant quest for fame and glory has, in fact, been a carefully orchestrated smokescreen. Think about it. What do you *really* know about me? Exactly. Nothing.

This is my story. You'll laugh, you'll cry, you'll run up and down some stairs for reasons that you don't quite understand and by the end, you'll probably feel as though you can fly. Well you can't, so don't bother trying.

Think about it – what do you **really** know about me? Exactly – nothing.

Medical research aspects
Sensational discovery

4

Best healthy eating advice
Which one is effective?

7

264/37

Today
28 °F / -2°C 56% Fair

WOOLLY LIFE

TICS · ECONOMICS · SCIENCE · ENGINEERING · MEDICINE · INDUSTRY · ECOLOGY · TECHNOLOGY

CULTURE

WOOLLY ACTING COMMUNITY UP IN

The woolly acting communi
this week, demanding equ
actors, regardless of
fury, feathered or sc
Monkey, who to
nothing until t
Hollywood
from f
we

TOP NEWS

MONKEY! MONKEY! MONKEY!

Monkey business is booming - we get the inside scoop.

NEWS

**REVEALS ALL
AHAMAS.**

ted enjoying a well-earned respite in a
resort in the Bahamas this week and the
s happy to show off his newly-toned physique.
so spent the better part of the afternoon posing for
n a cocktail in his hand, has clearly been working
e paparazzi snapped him buying 12 steak slices and
ets of crisps from a well-known high street pastry shop.

A close personal friend of Monkey's allegedly told the press
that, "he has always been conscious about the way he looks
and he has been preparing for a new fitness video in which
he'll be juggling fatty food." Monkey's agent has informed us
that nothing has been confirmed, but if all goes to plan, the
video should be in all good retailers at the end of the year.

ted a new range of silk lounge-wear
this week, which he has designed in collaboration with
top Saville Row tailors. The collection is designed to help
actors relax and unwind following a performance on

COMIC RELIEF
presents
THE ULTIMATE
JELLY WRESTLING MATCH
KEITH
LEMON
VS.
HARRY
HILL
£20
ALL SEATS
RESERVED
MONKEY'S
GARAGE
JUN
22
DOORS
8PM

If you like it and it sells a trillion copies, I'll be more than happy to write another nine, or ten volumes of my memoirs. Keith Lemon and Harry Hill are currently planning to wrestle in jelly for the right to play me in the film version of this book.

May the best man win.

MEANWHILE
ON WITH MY STORY
642035

Mummy's Boy

–Chapter Two–

Family history

As you probably know, I'm notoriously private and have never spoken about my family background before. I've always believed that some parts of a superstar's life should be kept away from the spotlight and that is what I have tried to do with my complex family history.

Or, at least, that was my stance until the Publisher informed me that if I wrote this autobiography, I would get to do a book-signing session in one of London's biggest stores.

Hmmm…

I demanded there be a red carpet, champagne, exquisite chocolates and that I'd get to sit in the same chair that Coleen Rooney had when she did her book signing. We finally agreed on most of those points and I'm looking forward to seeing the carpet.

It's traditional in autobiographies that the author spends some time at the start, recounting interesting tales of their distant relatives. I've read them all and I know how it goes.

Did you know that Geri Halliwell's second cousin's brother's wife's doctor's long-lost grandmother's twin sister was the world nun-wrestling champion for three decades? Oh, yes. Trufax. She left a trail of destruction in the gymnasiums of churches, nunneries and hospitals around the world. Her signature move was known as the 'Wimple Waster'. It chills me even to think about it.

When it comes to my own family background, my story is just as incredible. My parents owned a toy shop, but times were hard and they were forced to close it down in 1982.

My father had ordered a batch of 10,000 cheap Rubik's Cubes from Taiwan, but when they arrived, he discovered that all the coloured stickers were on the inside and it was impossible to use them. The fact that they also sprayed poisonous water everywhere whenever you tried to take them apart didn't help much either.

That was the final straw. No wait, the final straw was actually a board game called, *The Final Straw*, which had rules that were impossible to follow. He ordered 5,000 of those.

As my parents were clearing away and throwing out what was left of the stock, my mother came across me, stuck behind a pile of empty cardboard boxes. I was tatty, covered in dust and one of my ears was hanging off, but he couldn't bring herself to throw me away with all of the other rubbish.

She took me home and painstakingly restored me back to my former glory – cleaning me, re-stuffing me and sewing me up. Her love for me was so great that I amazingly found myself able to move and speak. My mother said that it was the most emotional moment of her life.

My first words to her? Ah… they were, quite simply, "Put the kettle on, eh Mum? I'm parched".

She says that, within minutes, I was demanding toast and then biscuits. And then trifle. And then cake. And then a bubble bath. And then a tree house. And then a BMX bike. All this in the hour before bedtime. A fully formed little character. The fledgling version of the magnificent woollen legend that you all know and love today.

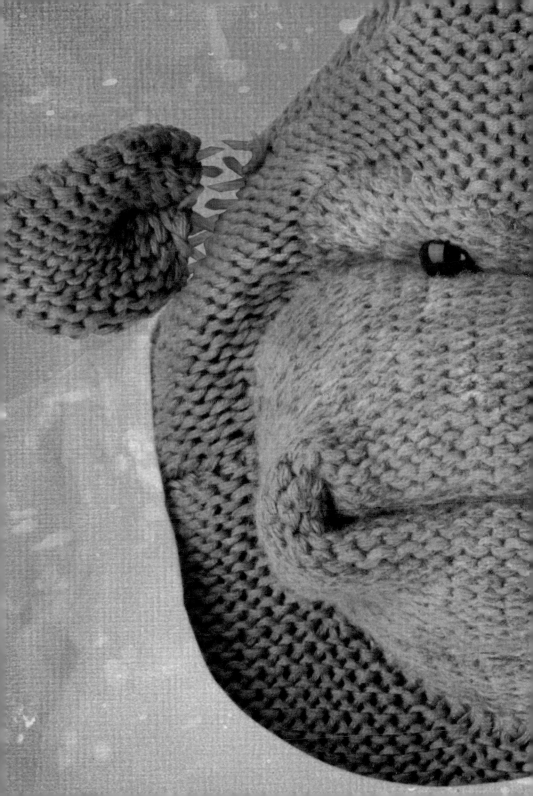

MR. DAWSON
IS A █████

—Chapter Three—

SCHOOL YEARS

BOOK THREE

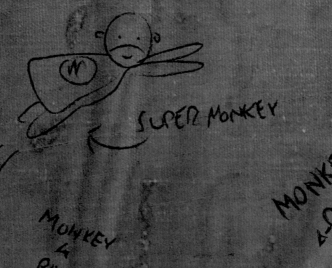

SUPER MONKEY

MONKEY
&
BMC

MONKEY ♡ MRS. DEVONSHIRE

STU. WOZ ERE

I know how celebrity autobiographies are usually filled with hard-luck tales from their childhoods. Stories about how they grew up living in a wooden crate with eleven brothers and sisters, sharing cold custard and only being allowed to wear socks every other Thursday. Sir Michael Caine, I am looking at you, and my heart will always bleed for you.

Dear reader, my life was no different. I will spare you some of the more horrendous details, not because I feel that it will be too much for you, but because it would make a much better, separate book to this one. And a film. And maybe a slightly weird musical. And probably a borderline illegal fairground ride as well.

I attended a normal school, just like all the other local children. There weren't any wool-only schools back then and I had to try to hold a pencil in my soft, delicate hands and write, just like all the other kids. It wasn't easy.

Then there were the desks. Sure, they were all designed for small children, but I was a mere eight inches tall back then and could barely see over the top of the desk. The teachers would stack up cushions for me to sit on, but I would invariably topple off them on to the floor, much to the delight of the evil human children who I thought were my friends.

Reader, I have a confession to make to you. As a schoolboy, I was beaten. I was beaten both severely and repeatedly.

I was beaten at chess, draughts, swingball, and, on occasion, ping-pong. It was awful, a tremendous blow to my confidence. It's a wonder that I turned into the talented, high-achieving, magnificent, modest individual whose exploits you're reading right now.

I strengthened my character by taking part in lots of activities and indulging in a whole host of hobbies. I joined my local woollen Scout troop and spent lots of time outdoors, camping, making fires and fishing.

Except for when it was raining. We couldn't go outdoors then, as we would all get soaked through and there's nothing less effective than a troop of soggy Scouts.

I was an only child and spent a lot of time playing alone in my bedroom with my large collection of toys. Some of them were larger than me, which was a bit intimidating, but I enjoyed myself most of the time.

THE AMAZING
MONKEY
WATCH IN AWE AS HE PUTS
HIS HEAD IN HIS OWN MOUTH
MAR.30

At school, I was able to keep the bullies away thanks to my natural ability to entertain and amuse. Not only was I a gifted joke teller, but thanks to my boneless woollen body, I was also able to put my entire head inside my own mouth.

I defy anyone not to find that kind of thing totally hilarious. Except for Simon Cowell, who strictly forbade me from going on *Britain's Got Talent* and doing it for the nation. As did Sir Bruce Forsyth, who strictly forbade me from doing it on *Strictly* as well. Don't know what's wrong with these people.

Because of my unusual appearance, from an early age, total strangers would point, stare and laugh at me in the street, so it was no surprise when I sought out the spotlight of fame and fortune. I figured that if I was going to be pointed, stared and laughed at, it would be better to earn a tidy sum of money while it was happening.

And lo, my magnetic attraction towards showbusiness was born!

I made my TV debut in the front row of the crowd of the World Snooker Championships in 1993. Ronnie O'Sullivan hit a shot so hard that the pink ball flew off the table and struck me on the forehead, knocking me out live on BBC2.

It was all over the newspapers and I became a minor celebrity. I saw this as my big chance to become a star and did every piece of showbusiness work that was offered to me.

I immediately left school, even though I was aged only 11. The headmaster raised no objections. He said that as I was a knitted toy, I probably shouldn't have been at the school in the first place, but he had been too polite to object to me being there.

After leaving school, I worked as a magician's assistant and a kids' entertainer. I even did summer seasons where I would sing the chart hits of the day, while gargling a mixture of water and washing-up liquid, before spraying an arc of bubbles over the delighted crowd.

On one occasion, I even flew all the way to Australia for a two-minute role on an Australian kids' show called *Ned's Barn* as Flora, the cheeky nun-monkey. I've still got the costume somewhere.

I learned my trade through non-stop work. I did a street theatre act that combined juggling and face-painting, worked on a couple of cruise liners and even had a stint in Bahrain working for the family of a prince. That ended badly when I realised I was allergic to sand and I swelled up to the size of a space hopper and floated away.

As a child star, my fame was fleeting. My voice broke and I fell victim to the teenager's curse. No, not acne – bobbling!

The nature of the work I was being offered changed. One year, the only job I could get was playing Choco, the cheeky clown-monkey puppet of a drunk ventriloquist on the northern club circuit. Most of our gigs were in the communal areas of old folks' homes and the audience regularly showed their displeasure by throwing their false teeth at us. When false teeth turned to bed pans, I took it as a literal sign that my career was heading down the toilet.

It was time to change course. It was time for me to become a 'proper actor'.

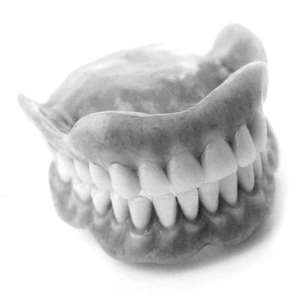

–*Chapter Four*–

THE EARLY STRUGGLE FOR FAME

As I'm sure you've heard it said before, the path to fame and glory is long and winding, like a meandering country lane, but with a pot of gold waiting for you at the foot of a rainbow, once you reach the end of the road.

Or, maybe you haven't heard it said before. To be honest, it's a phrase that I've only ever heard *major* celebs say to each other, so there's every chance that it'll be new to you. Trust me though, that's what it's like.

If you were to look at me now, you'd struggle to imagine that the proud, confident, cocky Monkey that adorns this wonderful book was once a shy, nervous wannabe. But it's true.

As I started out on the bottom rung of the showbiz ladder, I was a quivering wreck. Failing one audition after another owing to my inability to say my name without stammering, or fainting, or, as happened on one occasion, knocking myself out by walking the wrong way into a revolving door.

Don't laugh – we've all done it.

NEW Long Distance Course of Many Confidences

AMAZING New Way to be Confident.

FRIENDS! LADIES! BOYS! MEN! GIRLS! MONKEYS! Are you sick of that sinking feeling of 'I'm such a moron',' I must be better at life', 'I must think before I open my mouth, in the tropical insect house?' Well, silly people, you can be helped. You are not destined to lead the life of a waif and stray.

We'll help you discover what your self-belief blockage is and crush it with this simple to follow course. The **long distance course of many confidences**, consists of pioneering long distance telephone lessons that definitely work. By the end of the course you be more confident than a two legged man in a one legged race.

This course will help you; stand up yourself; win every argument; overcome a mental breakdown; understand how people's eyes work; feel comfortable meeting people in the nude; and deal confidently and calmly with milking a cow.

Just imagine a life free of worry, safe in the knowledge you'll always the right thing. You'll know exactly what to do and when to do it, you'll be perfect. WOW! Did we just say 'you'll be perfect'? YES. WE. DID.

There has never been an offer like this and we are fairly confident that there never will be again. We are dealers in truth and honesty, so believe us when we say this is one bona fide deal. You would be crazy to miss out. Signing up to this course, will be the most confident thing you do today, if ever.

Pioneering long distance confidences course is most recommended by Dr Phillip Bamgboshe.

In order to commence with the courses we as that you fill out the following information an return to the provided address along with th transfer of $65,000

Name ....
D.O.B. ....
Acc no. ....
Sort code. ....
Card no. ....
Pin no. ....
Exp Date .... (*required

It is with great pleasures that we entrust unto y of confidence.

Return to: Huts 6-11, 1st floor, 12, Samal Micro Astana 01003-0, Republic of Kazakhstan

I knew that if I was going to become the global superstar that I was destined to be, I would probably have to stop fainting and walking into doors all the time. So, I signed up for a distance-learning confidence course, where I would be sent my coursework through the post.

I sent off the $65,000 enrolment fee and waited.

And waited.

And waited.

After a year, I realised that I had been tricked. The confidence-boosting course did not exist – it was all a scam. The trouble was that I was so lacking in confidence that I didn't have the nerve to ring up to complain and demand my money back. I had been tricked. Tricked by scallywags.

I knew that I needed to become more confident. I saw a job advert in the window of my local department store, 'Santa Claus Wanted' and I knew that was the showbiz break I needed.

I strode right in there, my voice faltering and a little bit squeaky, but my nerves were steady. "I am the Santa Claus that you've been looking for!" I announced, only for the store manager to laugh so hard, the force of his laughter knocked me backwards.

This wasn't going to be easy. We entered into some tough negotiations – I demanded a two-hour working day with an hour for lunch and three times the going rate in pay. He came back with a counter-offer – I could sit on a shelf in the grotto, not move and pretend to be one of the children's gifts.

There was no way I was going to settle for humiliation like that and the negotiations went on for many more minutes before we agreed that, yes, I would sit on the grotto shelf and not move, but that I'd be allowed to wear a little Santa suit. Also, I would be allowed to take on the official role of Santa if Santa and all of his five stand-in replacements were off sick at the same time.

It felt like a huge win, even if I did spend most of the time being teased by the elves, who would get their kicks from throwing their soft, curly toed shoes at me. The tiny fiends.

Big Smoke

Power

Fame

Money

Success

China White

Lorraine Kelly

Flushed with confidence, and a small amount of money in my pocket, I decided that my next move on the road to fame and fortune would be to get some proper training and sign up for an acting school in London!

Working as one of the toys on the shelf of a grotto doesn't pay all that well and the only course I could afford to enrol on was at the barely famous, Hackney School of Moustache Acting.

It's a school that teaches young hopefuls how to act while wearing a variety of false moustaches. None of the usual singing, dancing, or learning and delivering lines kind of thing. This course was designed for the kind of actor that only wanted roles where they stood around in the background while wearing a false moustache.

I took to it like a duck to water and my tutor said that I wore a moustache with an intensity that he hadn't seen since Marlon Brando starred in *On The Waterfront*. I sought out a copy of the film only to find that Brando didn't have a moustache in it, but I'm sure my tutor knew what he was talking about. Weirdly, when I went back to the Hackney School of Moustache Acting, it was closed down.

I assumed that it meant that I had graduated. Hooray! Nothing could stop me now.

Selleck

Dali

Chaplin

Hogan

55

–Chapter Five–

ACHIEVING SHOWBIZ SUCCESS

Once I had conquered the admittedly small world of moustache acting, the natural progression was to move on to acting without a moustache. For some thespians, this can take years and years of training, but not for me. I just binned my collection of over 3,000 false moustaches and got on with it.

One moustache was saved though, as I needed it for a special mission. I found out where the head of the top acting school, RADA, lived and decided to pay her a special visit.

DISCLAIMER

I should point out that stalking laws were a lot looser back then and what I did was perfectly acceptable. Having said that, don't copy me. In fact, don't copy ANYTHING that I do. I'm me and you're not, and there's a strong chance that you'll just end up looking silly.

I donned the last remaining moustache and knocked on the door of Dame Lady Rada. I'm pretty sure that was her name (it isn't *that* important is it?) I pretended to be the window cleaner, there to collect my money. "Wotcha, madam," I said, in my best Cockney accent. "Window cleaner, here. That'll be two bob tuppence, ten farthings and a shilling, please."

She looked confused, but she fell for my ruse, hook, line and sinker, handing over a twenty pound note and telling me to keep the change.

I carefully removed the moustache and, a few moments later, I knocked on the door again. When Dame Lady Rada answered, I asked her if she recognised me.

Of course, she didn't! My cunning disguise had bewildered her completely. I reattached the moustache and re-adopted my super-convincing Cockney accent before roaring, "It is I, your Cockney window cleaner. Or should I say Monkey, arguably the greatest actor of this, or any other, generation!"

As I said, times were different a few years ago and whereas in this day and age she would have pressed some kind of panic button and alerted the police, her reaction was perfectly understandable – she fainted in my arms.

When she came to, she confessed that she'd never seen such a chameleon-like performance since Sir John Gielgud had played a chameleon in a children's TV show called, *Colin The Chameleon*. A show that never actually made it on to the air as the powers-that-be refused to believe that the role of Colin was being played by an actor, as opposed to a talking chameleon.

Sir John

TO BE... OR NOT TO BE...

She also asked me to marry her, but as she was 86 and I was, erm, considerably younger, I politely declined. That part was a bit weird.

Dame Lady insisted that I get put straight on to RADA's fast-track course for Hollywood Stardom the very next day. It's a bit like an intensive course of driving lessons and you can go from being a nobody to a major somebody in just a few days.

All the Brit stars who became 'overnight Hollywood sensations' have been on the course. Keira Knightley, Robert Pattinson, Hugh Grant. Mind you, Hugh bunked off on the afternoon of the 'Avoiding a Massive Scandal' lecture.

Those few days were the most exhausting that I've ever known, as I learned everything there is to know about the acting game.

Walking, staring, staring while walking, entering a room, exiting a room, staring across a room and kissing. Although, I only got to practise that last one on a loofah that had a face painted on it.

OH ROMEO, WHEREFORE ART...

I'M HERE

When the RADA course ended, I was bundled on a plane and sent straight to Hollywood, where a rabid gang of paparazzi were there to greet me upon my arrival.

I was prepared for this and chose to wear a pair of shades and a mankini for the occasion. They'd literally never seen anything like it before. Within days, I was the talk of Hollywood, appearing at all the biggest showbiz parties and being spotted with top celebrities or, if it was the stars' night off, their lookalikes.

The milkshake flowed and the ladies threw themselves at me. I had so many women who wanted to sell kiss-and-tell stories about me that I had to schedule appointments for them all.

In among all of the fame and fortune, I even managed to find time to do some acting and quickly established myself as the go-to guy for any director who was looking for a small, woollen, slightly nervous actor.

6am — Workout with Arny at
       GOLDS GYM

7am — Meet Jay K for
       Smoothie + gos

8am — Pap opportunity 📷
         with Angelina

09.00 — Hobnob with
         Madonna

10.00 — Pap opportunity ♡♡
     with Mila Kunis   ♡

11.00 — Sell my Pamela Anderson
             Kiss and tell.

12.00 — Wet lunch with
       Spielberg 🥤

13.00 - Go on George Michael's speed boat with all his lady friends :) :)

2pm - Sack manager

3pm - Hire Mr. T as manager

4pm - Afternoon tea with the Fresh Prince of Bel Air

5pm - Hit muscle beach with Stallone

6pm - Kiss + tell with Destiny's Child

7pm - Massage (by Phoebe from friends)

8pm

Hit the Beverly night club in west Hollywood for exclusive night with Cher. (wear best aftershave)

Some people have said that I was all about the hype and that I neglected my talent by appearing in any old trash that I was offered. To that I say, tish and fipsy!

You should try telling the actors and hard-working crew that came together to make *Spy Shark Prison Escape 7* that their work is all a load of meaningless fluff. Most of the ones that are still alive will argue very strongly with you indeed.

In case you haven't had the pleasure of seeing it, *Spy Shark Prison Escape 7* was a marvellous film in which I played Dusty Fresh, a hip-hop singer who had been imprisoned after rapping rude words in his sleep. Viewers were kept guessing whether I was a spy, or shark, right until the end of the film. If you're one of the few people who hasn't seen it, I won't spoil the ending here.

STRAIGHT TO
VHS
STARRING
MONKEY
AS
"DUSTY FRESH"
SPY SHARK
PRISON ESCAPE
7
"A SEMINAL AQUA BASED, ESPIONAGE, GENRE BENDING CLASSIC"
★★★★★

If you asked any cinema expert what my finest role was, they'd almost certainly say it was, Thirteenth Man To Emerge From Hole, in the classic straight-to-VHS movie, *35 Men and a Hole* – the made-up story of an actual mining disaster. In the film, 35 men were trapped when their mine collapsed and the story focuses on their attempts to survive and their eventual rescue.

I didn't have a speaking part. There were just too many men and the hole wasn't all that big, but my role as Thirteenth Man To Emerge From Hole was crucial. After seeing twelve men coming out of the hole, there would be a chance that the audience might start to become bored with it all. So, man number thirteen had to offer something different in order to hold the viewers' attention.

I didn't disappoint. As I emerged from the hole, squinting in the sunlight after a month underground, I improvised and whipped my trousers off, waved them around my head and yelled, "Shirley, I'm coming home, baby!"

At the wrap party, the director told me that my performance had saved the film. "Monkey," he wept, "guys ten, eleven and twelve almost killed the vibe stone dead. Every one of them crying and falling to their knees, as they came out of that damn hole. But not you. You went for comedy and it was your trouser-waving that lifted the audience and made them want to sit through the sight of another 22 men coming out of a hole."

It was to be my last major Hollywood role. There was no way I could beat it, so it was time to do something new. Sport.

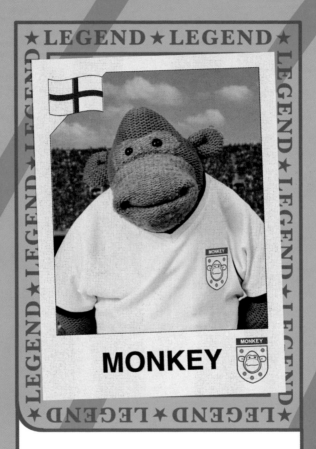

MONKEY

Legend factoid: Legs too weak to actually run, let alone kick a ball.

–Chapter Six–

★ LEGEND ★ LEGEND ★
LEGEND

LEGEND
LEGEND

LEGEND

LEGEND
LEGEND
★ LEGEND ★ LEGEND ★

06

MY SPORTING PROWESS

Just what is it that has made me the global success story that I undoubtedly am? Why, it's my versatility.

Not only did I crack the tricky world of acting and general showbiz almost overnight, I also thrived in the world of sport. Or to be more precise – woolly sport.

I've always been something of a fitness fanatic. I can do star jumps, running up and down stairs, and I once threw a hot sausage roll over a house when it burnt my fingers.

With all of those skills in my locker, it was only a matter of time before I was asked to take part in the Woollen Games and when I did, I was soon smashing records like a bull in a… erm, record shop.

I was lucky enough to be asked to carry the Woollen Games flag during the opening ceremony. Some people said that I'd refused to take part unless I was afforded that prestigious honour, but they know who they are and they're liars.

When I catch up with them, they'll be getting their big mouths zipped *permanently*, but that's not really important right now.

I won gold medals in every one of the seventeen events that I took part in – mostly thanks to the coaching help I received from my many celebrity chums.

In football, my good friend David 'Goldenballs' Beckham, jumped at the opportunity to help me out with my silky skills, even though they were already pretty silky to begin with.

In fact, I remember Becks saying, "Monkey, even my wife's silkiest underwear isn't as silky as your silky skills." Then he got a bit embarrassed and there was an awkward silence, before we carried on practising free kicks until it got dark.

When it came to the tennis, I first asked Andy Murray to coach me, but his non-stop joking and pranking on the court meant that we got nothing done. That man is a walking LOL-athon.

In the end, I had to let him go and recruited Venus and Serena Williams to coach me instead. I insisted that they play against me at the same time and figured that if I could beat two of the world's best players at once, I shouldn't have any problems against Bagpuss.

You know what? I was right. Another gold medal chalked up for Monkey.

In the rowing, I enlisted Sir Steve Redgrave to show me the ropes, which he duly did. Unfortunately, you row a boat with oars and not ropes, so I had to get him to come back for another coaching session. "I told you it was oars and not ropes!" I shouted at him. Or maybe he shouted it at me. My memory is a little bit hazy on that one.

For the downhill sledging, I called upon the talents of Tiger Woods. Yes, I know he's a golfer, but I don't know any top sledgers and I had a hunch that Tiger might be an expert. I was wrong – he was hopeless, but I still won the gold. It turns out that not many woolly characters like to do the sledging. They don't like it when they fall off – they get all wet and have to spend a couple of hours drying off on the radiator afterwards.

I like to think that it was my presence that helped to make the Woollen Games the roaring success that it was and if it wasn't for me, the next Games (currently scheduled to go ahead in 2036) almost certainly wouldn't be happening.

–*Chapter Seven*–

As you probably know, I haven't just written this book in order to win all the literary awards and be invited on to important TV arts programmes, where I will get to stroke my chin and say, "Hmmm," and, "Aaaahhh," and, "Oh yes, I see what the sculptor was trying to do there and it works for me on *so* many levels." Although, I'm pretty sure that all of that kind of stuff will happen.

No, this book has been made so the lovely little people at Comic Relief can fund themselves. In fact, I've acted as a consultant to the lovely red-nosed folk's fund-raising efforts right from the start. It was me who suggested that they change their special celebration to Red Nose Day from Red Toes Day, after I pointed out that not everyone would want to wear flip-flops, or go barefoot in March.

It was also my idea that the red noses should be detachable, so that they wouldn't have to be worn forever. Someone (I'm naming no names, but it was Lenny Henry) had the bright idea that everyone should have their noses turned red, permanently, with bright red dye, or tattoo ink.

We had an explosive row over that one, which ended up in the car park with me and Lenny wrestling in the gravel and shouting abuse at each other. We're good friends now, or at least I expect we will be, once his restraining order comes to an end in 2027.

One of my Comic Relief roles is to sit on the committee that decides which activities are to be classed as fun and which aren't.

For example:

Baked bean bath =
FUN

Climbing up chimney =
NOT FUN

3-legged race up hill =
FUN

Rolling down hill in barrel =
NOT FUN

We had a lot of trouble agreeing on that chimney one – again, Lenny Henry and I almost came to blows over it. It was all sorted once I insisted that he spent twelve hours in a chimney himself to see how he liked it.

Another short wrestle in the gravel later, and everything was smoothed out. Apart from the gravel – that wasn't smooth, not even in the slightest. Actually, it's just occurred to me that perhaps Lenny enjoys picking fights with me, solely so that he can wrestle in the gravel in the Comic Relief car park.

I think I'll need to add 'Wrestling with Monkey in the gravel in the Comic Relief car park' on the end of the list of things that are classed as being 'not fun'.

I like to get completely involved when it comes to my Comic Relief work – unlike some celebrities that I could name – but of course that would be uncharitable. They know who they are. Sending along a friend who is wearing a celebrity cardboard face mask will *never* be acceptable in the fund-raising game.

One of my all-time favourite charity events was with the Spice Girls. This was back when they were just starting out and would do anything to get their pictures in the pa... erm, I mean, back when they were completely devoted to good causes and raising money for charity. As they still are and always will be. I hope that's not going to be a problem for the lawyers.

Our task was to try and raise £5,000 by doing a non-stop dance routine that would last for 500 minutes. That's almost eight and a half hours. Yes, I know. Completely unacceptable.

The girls were younger and fitter than I was and so I needed to try and keep up with them. After the first half an hour, I was exhausted. However, I soon realised that I could still be part of the dance routine, even if I wasn't doing any actual dancing. I spent the rest of the time hopping from the shoulder of one Spice Girl to the next, resting on them as they carried the burden and danced their little hearts out.

Of course, I made it look as though I was giving it the full-monty and did lots of finger-snapping, head-nodding and jazz hands for the duration.

We completed the challenge, raised the money and only four of the five Spice Girls needed extensive physiotherapy afterwards, so everyone was a winner.

Speaking of the full-monty, my other most notable charity stunt was

REMOVED BY LAWYERS ON GROUNDS OF DECENCY.

CENSORED

**MONKEY'S
SCHOOL OF SHOWBUSINESS**

Kerry Katona BA (hons)

has sucessfully accomplished
showbiz superstardom and is
now qualified to be papped
and drink in the Ivy.

Signed by

Chapter Eight

HOW TO BECOME A SHOWBIZ SUPERSTAR

1. Know your specialist area. If you are a singer, don't paint. If you are an actor, don't play football. If you're Al, put the kettle on eh?

2. There is no number two. You don't need to know why.

3. It's all about the (audience) You might think that making a short film about the secret life of a worm that lives in the shed of an old woman is interesting. It isn't. People want to see car chases, kisses, and explosions. Never forget that.

4. An autograph hunter is just a stalker with stationery. Handle with extreme caution.

5. Never turn down any work. One day you might realise that you have been 'between jobs' for two years and that film about the superhero octopus that wears enchanted eight-legged jeans that you thought you were too good for might not seem like such a bad idea after all.

6. <u>Always</u> be modest, no matter how hard it might be. This is a really tough one, believe me.

7. Practice, practice, practice – it's the only way you'll get to the top of your chosen career. If for some reason you're not practicing, you should be practicing your practicing.

8. Spend as much time with your friends as you can, before you become famous. Once you're a star, you'll drop them all like a handful of hot pebbles, but if you put the effort in now, they'll hate you less in the future. :)

9. There is no number nine. It's notoriously bad luck in showbiz. Like saying the name of that Scottish play, or working with animals or children.

10. You'll never be big enough to have your own personal, private zoo. The day you think you are, you've lost it. It's over.

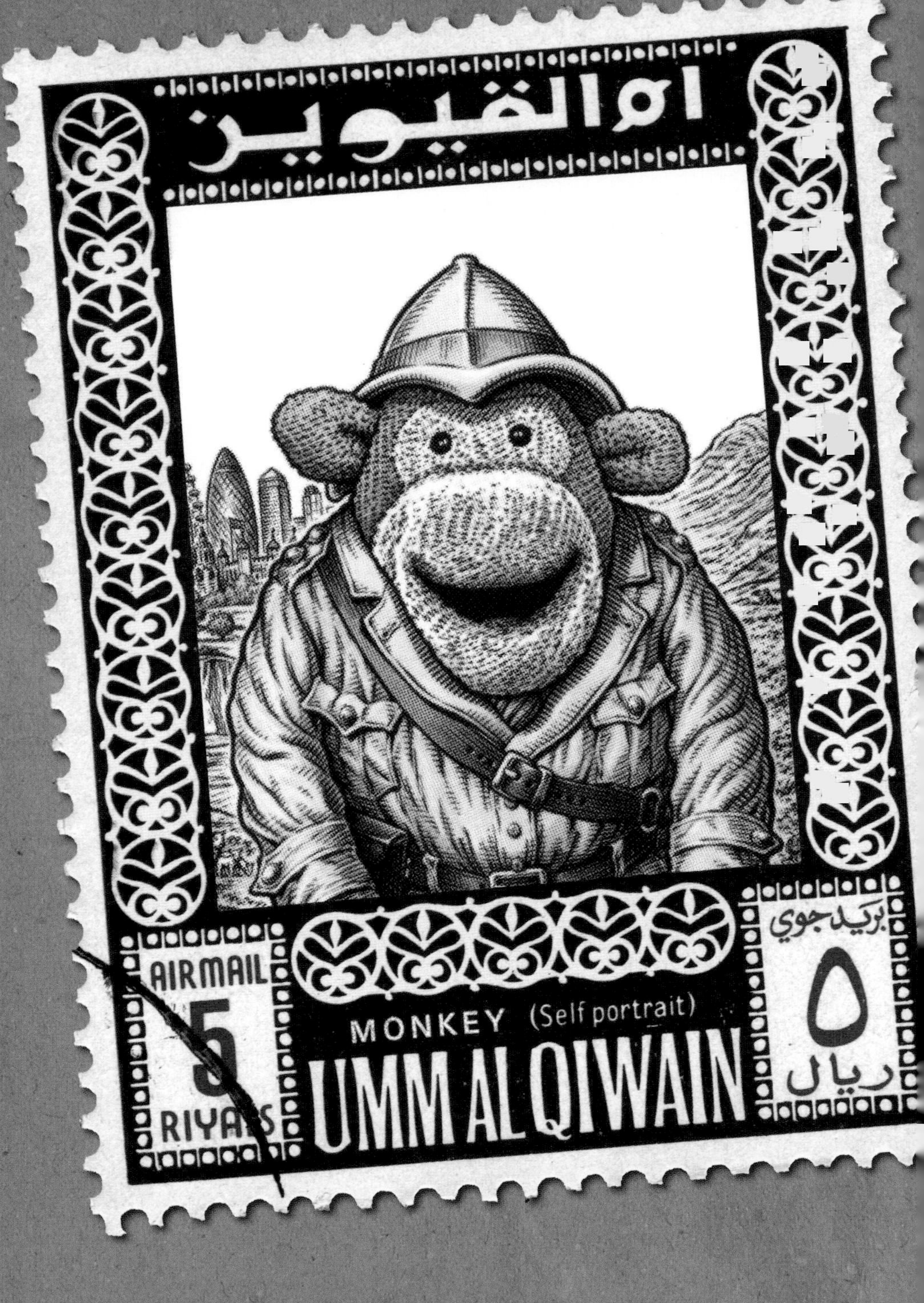
ام القيوين
AIRMAIL
5
RIYALS
بريد جوي
٥
ريال
MONKEY (Self portrait)
UMM AL QIWAIN

AIR PAR AVION MAIL

–Chapter Nine–

ME AS A
FEARLESS
EXPLORER

RUGGED OUTDOOR ADVENTURES

When I'm not being amazing and famous, I like to unwind by being amazing in private, out of the public eye.

It's good, because (a) it helps me to stay amazing, which is very important and (b) I don't always have to wash my hair, which is the worst part about bath night and means I can spend more time playing with my ducks, which of course is also amazing. In fact, let's all just pause for a moment and reflect on how amazing I am.

There. That was nice wasn't it?

Over the past few years, I've become a fearless explorer and adventurer, but I don't like to get any publicity for it, in case some of my loyal fans try to copy me and get seriously injured.

One of my biggest fans is that Bear Grylls from off the telly. In fact, it was me who first inspired Bear to get out into the wild and start eating bugs and drinking pond water, like he does. Bear once asked if he could join me on a trek along the Pyrenees that I was planning. It was a particularly tricky trek, as I had decided to do the whole thing with a pair of underpants on my head. It started off well and we got the bus from my house to the train station with no major problems, but once we were on the train, en-route to the foot of the Pyrenees, things started to go a bit wrong.

The seats that Bear had reserved online were both facing backwards and Bear said that travelling in reverse made him feel weird. The train was full and there were no other available seats, so Bear had no option but to get off at the next station and head back home.

I tried not to laugh at him, but it was tough.

I carried on and did my tricky trek on my own, getting a big medal for brilliance when I'd finished. Bear says that, to this day, he still can't put a pair of underpants on his head, as it's too traumatic.

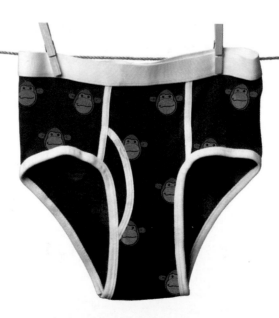

"The first woolly ascent of The Pyrenees (with pants on head)"

My favourite Lederhosen

Milking it!

The Channel tunnel expedition

Delta Force M...

As an adventurer, I've pretty much done it all and have been everywhere you could possibly imagine – up the Nile, down the Alps, round the Hanging Gardens of Babylon, through the Channel Tunnel and across the wide high street of Stockton-On-Tees.

Surviving the great storm of '04

Grand Master Mon Kei

Nothing scares me – not even pirates. A few years ago, while I was sailing around the world backwards, in a washing machine during a few weeks off, I successfully fought off a gang of ruthless pirates.

They caught me whilst I was napping, boarded the washing machine by hooking their ropes on to the powder dispenser and woke me with a start. At first, I thought they were going to rob me, but they just wanted to know if I wanted to buy any DVDs of the latest cinema releases, which they had in a suitcase.

Okay, so they may not have been the most ruthless pirates on the high seas, but I stood firm and they left empty-handed.

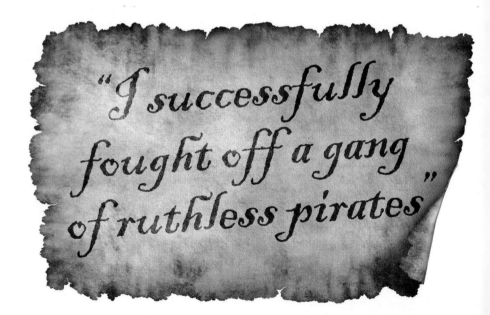

"I successfully fought off a gang of ruthless pirates"

Then there was the time I came across a previously undiscovered tribe, deep in the heart of the rainforest. Naturally, they were delighted to see me and once I'd persuaded them not to kill me and eat me, we all got along swimmingly.

They were living amongst a massive crop of tea plants and were completely oblivious to their value. When I pitched up, they were burning the tea leaves and mixing the ashes with water to make grey lipstick for their cattle.

I soon put them right and after a short demonstration, they were all brewing and enjoying tea, as I bade them farewell and continued on with my travels. The cattle didn't look very happy about any of it, mind you.

Plus, if I was to tell you about my close friendship with the Dalai Lama, about how I'm the first number on his speed dial, how he consults me on an everyday basis (Daily Lama more like – ha!) and how he keeps begging me to get him a leading role in a Woody Allen film, you'd probably think I was being arrogant. So I won't.

The ITV Digital days

–Chapter Ten–

MY ADVERTISING
WORK & MEETING AL

As I became more and more famous, my life changed and, almost overnight, loads of offers of advertising work were being thrown at me.

Suddenly, big companies were knocking on my door, begging me to appear in adverts for their products. They'd taken a close look at this most famous monkey and realised that he was a potential gold mine.

Plus, of course, I have a voice that you can trust and a face that could melt the hardest slab of butter. Or is it the other way round? Hmmm… perhaps it's neither.

Floods of requests would come into my office every day. "Monkey, will you advertise our bank?", "Monkey, will you advertise our fish-flavoured crisps?", "Monkey, will you advertise this wi-fi garden hose?" Fortunately, I believe in doing my research and I quickly discovered that wi-fi garden hoses aren't actually a thing.

After a lot of thought and consideration and doing some complicated sums, I decided that I should lend my support to a small company called ITV Digital. It was helpful, as they said they would film the commercial in my house – *very* important.

Fish 'n' Crisp

NEW!

Fish flavoured crisps

This pack contains

Calories	Sugar	Fat	Saturates	Salt
1981	11.4g	20.1g	5.7g	7.2g
90%	85%	95.7%	99.9%	201.3%

of an adult's guideline daily amount

150g

On the day of filming, there was a knock at the door, half an hour before anyone was supposed to arrive. A portly young man stood before me and tried to sell me some dusters. As I collect dusters (I have over 19,000 in a storage unit close to my home), I invited him in and made him a cup of tea while he showed me his range of brightly coloured cloths.

When the film crew arrived shortly afterwards, they brought my co-star with them, or rather, the guy they wanted to be my co-star. I wasn't impressed. He was tall, dark, handsome and had soft, delicate hands. I knew straight away that he wouldn't be suitable to play alongside me in this important advert.

No, no. This attractive, charming young actor was only going to look *foolish* when acting alongside myself. It wouldn't be fair on him. I insisted that he be dismissed from the project at once and replaced with the bumbling door-to-door duster salesman, who by this point had got his hand trapped in my cookie jar.

There followed a slight difference of opinion between myself and the film crew, which included me spending a lengthy period of time locked in the cupboard under the stairs. Six hours later, we were all sorted and myself and Al were an on-screen duo for the first time.

Of course, ITV Digital disappeared shortly afterwards. Although that was *nothing* to do with the work of Al and myself (we have very good lawyers, in case you were thinking of suggesting that it did).

Shortly afterwards, we were lucky enough to be snapped up by PG tips for what was a world-record transfer fee at the time – a year's supply of tea for myself and a bucket of sherbet for Al.

There were a few problems at first. The chimps that used to be in the PG Tips ads weren't happy and I think they were responsible for a lot of silent phone calls that I used to get in the middle of the night. Not to mention the scores of pizzas that were ordered and delivered to my home, where I was expected to pay for them upon delivery. It was obviously the work of the chimps, as all of the pizzas were topped with bananas.

These days, I prefer to have total creative control over the adverts that I appear in. With some stars, it's a case of just turning up for an advert, saying the words that are in the script, doing exactly what the director asks you to do, and then going home again, filled with the satisfaction of a job well done.

I'm not like that. I like to give back much, much more and get involved in every single part of the advertising process. However, even though I like to have total creative control, some of my ideas don't always make it onto the small screen. In fact, now that I think about it, none of them have. Ever. Which is a bit strange.

With my PG Tips work, I like to visit the advertising agency when they're having meetings. Sometimes, they move the dates and times of the meetings and forget to tell me, which is quite frustrating.

One time, there was some kind of strange mix-up and I found myself in a meeting room with eight top, high-flying advertising executives. Or so I thought.

When I took a closer look and poked and prodded a couple of them, it turned out that they were actually broomsticks with balloons stuck on top. The balloons had wigs on and crudely-drawn faces. It was a simple mistake and one that anyone could have made. I was quite upset, but Al sat and chatted with them all for ages.

Al has been a near-constant companion ever since I first met him. I took the decision that having him around would be a lot like having a dog, but with the added bonus that (a) he'd be able to do all of his 'toilet stuff' on his own and in an actual toilet, and (b) there wouldn't be much shedding of hair.

Reader, I was half-right. I won't tell you on which one though.

He fetches me my slippers and newspaper when I ask him to, he only gets up on the sofa when I say he can, and he doesn't try to eat the ducks whenever he goes for a swim in the lake. So, I can't really complain, can I?

… IT TURNED OUT THAT THEY WERE ACTUALLY BROOMSTICKS WITH BALLOONS STUCK ON TOP. HA!

–Chapter Eleven–

LIFE AT THE TOP

N ow that I'm a globally recognised name and possibly
the most famous woollen star that has ever lived,
the question that I get asked most is, "Monkey, just
exactly what is it that you *do*?"

By that, I assume people are really trying to say,
"Tell us about your average day, in extreme detail,
so that we can try and understand what makes such
an amazing and enigmatic phenomenon tick."

It would be my pleasure to oblige,
but the truth is that there isn't really a typical
day for me. Life is a constant whirlwind,
with functions to attend, meetings to have and
genius ideas to be hatched.

But, as you've paid good money to read this book (unless you've got it from a library, in which case, *don't get sticky fingerprints on it!*) I feel I should indulge you all and let you in on the majestic wonderfulment that is my life.

A 'typical day' begins with me being woken by my alarm clock. It's a rare, 'double Swiss' clock. As you know, Swiss clocks are known for their precision, but mine was made in Switzerland to the highest standards, shipped to the UK and then sent back to Switzerland again, so that it could be made 'double Swiss'.

If there was such a thing as time on the moon, this clock could tell it as accurately as science will allow. Maybe there is time on the moon. I haven't been yet, so I don't know.

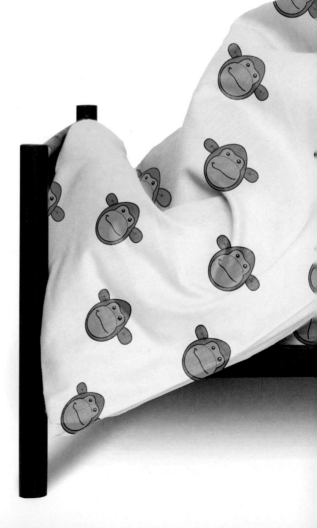

Breakfast usually consists of tea and toast. I like to keep as true to my roots as possible and even though I regularly get offered exotic items, such as quail eggs and unicorn bacon, I refrain from consuming them and stick to my tried and trusted breakfast routine.

After that, it's time to check my diary and when I'm happy that, yes, it's definitely my diary, I look inside it. It's usually full of things that I need to do, so I quickly close it again and head to my home gym.

Well, I say 'home gym', but it's actually some swings and a slide that I keep in my garage in case it rains. They're just as good as regular fitness equipment and a lot more fun, too.

While I'm exercising, my colleague Al reads out the morning papers to me. He struggles with some of the posh words in the big papers, and when that happens, I encourage him to act out what he can see in the pictures instead. It's a lot of fun for both of us – well, it definitely is for me.

As a reward, Al is allowed to have five minutes playtime on the swings and slide. I put that in because I know that some of you care about him and want to know that he's happy.

Unicorn Bacon

16 RASHERS

9 771473 968012 >

300g

130

It's a little-known fact that Hollywood doesn't open until the afternoon, so I follow up my physical exercise by working on my mental agility. I do this by playing on my games consoles, sometimes playing on six different ones at the same time.

I've got all of the popular consoles that you'll have heard of, plus three extra-special ones that only megastars are allowed to have – the WhizzBox, the Mega Fun 7 and the Game Potato. That last one is a console with a controller that looks like an ordinary potato, so if you ever see a paparazzi shot of Brad Pitt, or Beyonce, thumbing vigorously at a raw potato, they're actually playing a game.

I'm usually pretty exhausted after that and like to take a nap before lunch. I've got a special relaxation tape consisting of whale noises, which helps me drift off to sleep. It's actually whale impersonations, as recorded by Englebert Humpback, The Sperm Whales and Girls Aloud, especially for me.

It's the only time the groups have joined forces in the studio, so I'm lucky to have the tape. You should hear Cheryl Cole's impersonation of a birthing whale mother – it'd happily send anyone off to the land of nod.

WOW
WHALE NOISES!

Including the hits 'We love to sonar' by Englebert Humpback and '3 clicks and I'm yours' by The Sperm Whales

Lunch could be anything from a crisp sandwich to a three-crisp sandwich, and then it's time to get down to work, either calling up some of my Hollywood contacts, or having a video chat in the office that I've built for myself under the stairs.

For legal reasons, I can't say anything more about the projects that are in the pipeline. Some of them are with stars that aren't even famous yet, and if I told you their names, you'd scratch your head in puzzlement. Having said that, if I told you their names and you were reading this in 2018, then you'd be amazed.

Once work is over, I head off to one of the more elite restaurants in town. Sometimes it's the one that sells curly fries while other times, it'll be the one where I'm allowed to eat with my fingers.

My pre-bedtime routine is a cup of tea and a catch up with all the soap operas, mainly so that I can keep in touch with how ordinary people live. You do have a lot of dramas, don't you? It's mainly crime and tragedy with you lot, although sometimes you get married and have babies, too.

SOMETIMES I WISH MY LIFE WAS ORDINARY, LIKE THE PEOPLE IN SOAPS. BUT IT SOON PASSES.

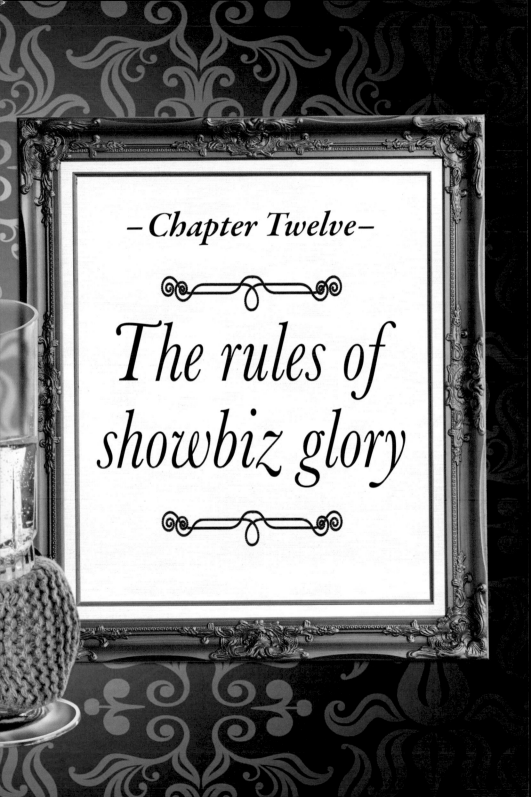

–Chapter Twelve–

The rules of showbiz glory

Every day, I receive about 300 letters from fans, all asking the same thing, "Monkey, how can I become as successful and amazing as you are?" Admittedly, 295 of them come from one particularly enthusiastic fan in Stockport, but it's still a very good question.

So, in an attempt to make the world a far better place by making everyone a bit more like me, on the next page are my rules of success. Follow each of these to the letter and you'll soon be as incredible as I am.

Dearest Monkey,

I love you. I love you so much. I love your little eyes, your lovely little ears and those funny little t-shirts you wear.

Don't ask me how I got it, but I sleep with a tuft of your wool underneath my pillow, so we will always be together when we sleep.

I really hope that someday we can be together. I sit patiently by the letterbox awaiting your reply,

Love your BIGGEST fan,
Pamela Anderson
xxxxxxx

PA + M
4 EVA
x

 **BE NICE TO EVERYONE.** THAT SHOP ASSISTANT THAT YOU'RE RUDE TO MIGHT BECOME YOUR BUTLER ONE DAY AND HE'LL SEEK REVENGE BY PUTTING CURRY POWDER IN YOUR CUSTARD.

 **PRACTISE.** THEY SAY THAT IT TAKES 10,000 HOURS OF DOING SOMETHING TO BECOME BRILLIANT AT IT. OR ONE HOUR TO BECOME BRILLIANT AT 10,000 THINGS, I CAN NEVER QUITE REMEMBER.

 **WORK HARD.** REMEMBER WHEN ROBBIE WILLIAMS STOPPED WORKING HARD? I KNOW, HORRIBLE WASN'T IT?

 **THERE IS NO RULE FOUR.** YOU DON'T NEED TO KNOW WHY.

 **LISTEN TO EVERY PIECE OF ADVICE** THAT YOU ARE GIVEN. HOWEVER, IF YOU THINK THE ADVICE IS SILLY, FEEL FREE TO LAUGH AT THE ADVICE-GIVER, POINT AT THEIR FACE AND SHOUT, "THAT'S RIDICULOUS!" THEY'LL VALUE YOUR FEEDBACK.

 **DEVELOP YOUR AUTOGRAPH.** DO ONE THAT HAS LOTS OF SWIRLS, BUT IS IMPOSSIBLE TO READ. ALL THE TOP STARS DO THOSE ONES.

 SEE RULE FOUR.

 **BE LOYAL TO YOUR FANS.** THEY ARE THE ONES WHO HAVE MADE YOU THE SUCCESS THAT YOU ARE. IF A FAN WANTS TO GIVE YOU A KISS ON THE CHEEK – LET THEM. IF THEY WANT TO GRAB YOUR LEG, AS YOU WALK DOWN THE STREET SO THAT YOU HAVE TO DRAG THEM ALONG THE PAVEMENT – CALL THE POLICE.

 **DON'T GET AN AGENT.** I'LL ADVISE YOU FOR HALF A PERCENT LESS THAN AN AGENT WOULD CHARGE YOU. TRUST ME, IT'S WORTH IT.

 EVEN IF YOU'RE NOT A SHOWBIZ SUCCESS, **PRETEND** THAT YOU ARE AND ACT ACCORDINGLY. IT MIGHT COST YOU ALL OF YOUR FRIENDSHIPS, BUT INSIDE YOU'LL FEEL AMAZING. THIS IS MY GOLDEN RULE.

–*Chapter Thirteen*–

THE FUTURE

So, there's my story. We've reached the present day, which means that it's only really the story so far. I know, it's been a tale of phenomenal success and you've probably had to stop reading a few times so that you could go for a lie down after it made you feel dizzy.

There's no doubt that there'll be many more volumes of my autobiography to come over the next few years, but what will be in them? Where does Monkey go from here? It's a very good question and one that I will try to answer for you.

Obviously, I've got many, many more acting projects in the pipeline, most of them in Hollywood. I might do one of those Scandinavian crime dramas, because everyone in them seems to wear nice jumpers and I look great in a lovely pullover.

Unfortunately, I can't talk about any of my top Hollywood projects right now. They're so hush-hush and top secret at the moment that even I don't know what they're about. Whenever I ring up the producers and directors that I'll be working with, they tell me that they can't tell me anything about the films we'll be making, and that that they'll call me back as soon as they've got some info.

In some cases, they don't even answer the phone at all. That's a bit weird, but that's how Hollywood works and you've got to learn to live with it.

I'll also be doing a lot more campaigning for actors like myself with the other members of the Woolly Actors Guild. You've almost certainly heard of us – we're fighting to get more roles for woolly actors in top films. We believe that all actors should be given equal employment opportunities, regardless of whether they are woolly, furry, feathered, or flesh.

Myself, Zippy, George, Bungle and Bagpuss – all the big names are part of the WAG – are not prepared to stop protesting until we're given joint billing with stars like Tom Cruise, Angelina Jolie and Christopher Biggins.

In fact, my work for equal woolly rights goes even further than that and I've got plans for a chain of high-class restaurants aimed at the woolly community as well. There'll be small plates and cutlery, low chairs and the kind of atmosphere that can only be knitted.

L'AUGUILLE D'OR

WAG
DIR: A. GINGER   CAM: G.M
ROLL   SLATE
2   5
DATE: 14 SEPT. 2011

The
Supporting
Hand Award

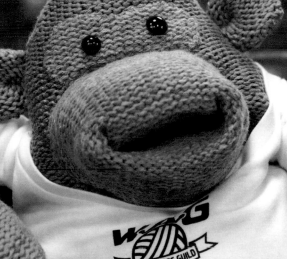

SEXIEST
CROCHET
& WEAVER
of the year
2007

Assisted Actor 1999

WAG
WOOLLY ACTORS GUILD

Of course, one day I'd love to settle down and start a family, which I'll need a wife for. It's nice to have Al around the place, but I see him as someone who is teaching me what it's like to have a child of my own. Hopefully, when that happens, my child won't be a giant, sweaty and slightly confused, like Al is, but you never know.

Long term, I think I see part of my future in the world of science. I'm a big fan of that man off the TV with the floppy hair who talks about the planets with an aura of mystical wonder. I'd quite like a piece of that action, but I'll need to go further. In fact, I'll need to go where no woollen celebrity has gone before. Yes, I'll need to go into actual space itself.

When I've got a spare moment or two, I'll be emailing NASA and asking if I can be the first woolly character to explore the far reaches of the solar system. I'm particularly keen to explore Mars, as I don't think anyone else has tried very hard so far. There's obviously Martians up there (we wouldn't have the word 'Martians' if there wasn't), but I reckon that they've been hiding behind some rock whenever a Mars probe has landed on the planet.

So, with that in mind, I think that by the time the next volume of my scintillating, exciting, jaw-dropping, breath-away-taking autobiography hits the shops, you'll be reading about how the Monkey who conquered Hollywood has also conquered Mars.

What could possibly go wrong?

With special thanks to

all the artists who appear in this book
for their on-going support for Comic Relief.

I'd also like to thank the following people for helping
me make this book as brilliant as... me!
Salvador Brown, Paul Randall, Rhian Ap Gruffydd,
Steve Teague, Jason Joyce, Ian Tuttle, Dave Hopkins,
Mark Waites, Andy Medd, Nick Hallbery, David Colman,
Amy Garret, Jenna Stamp, Hettie Rifkin,
Ben McNaughton, Steven Williams, George Lavender,
Patrick Larder, Andy Dawson and Mother.